Re-Creations

by Jean Starr Untermeyer

POETRY

Growing Pains
Dreams Out of Darkness
Steep Ascent
Winged Child
Love and Need
Later Poems
Job's Daughter

MEMOIRS

Private Collection

TRANSLATIONS

Schubert the Man (by Oscar Bie)
The Death of Virgil (by Hermann Broch)

Re-Creations

Translations by
Jean Starr Untermeyer

Foreword by Lewis Galentière

W · W · NORTON & COMPANY, INC ·
New York

This book is dedicated to four women:
Sylvia Townsend Warner
Valentine Ackland
Elizabeth Bosshart
Helen Teschner Tas
a fragrant wreath redolent of affection,
loyalty, music, and poetry.

Contents

Verses Set to Music

Foreword

Jean Starr Untermeyer was born with music in her heart, and in a time, more than eighty years ago, when music, in the United States, apart from Italian opera, meant German music. As a young girl, she prepared herself for the concert hall, studying at home and in Vienna, and in Vienna made her début as a concert singer. A passionate nature, a deep responsiveness to the dolors and exaltations of the human heart, and a powerful poetic imagination impelled her to creative rather than interpretive expression and made of her a poet.

Her place in American poetry has long been assured and her reputation crowned by her most recent collection, *Job's Daughter*. She has been, at the same time, a generous lover of the poetry of others, to the point of spontaneously expressing that love in creative translations of the foreign poets she has admired—mainly German, her second language, but French and Spanish as well. Meanwhile, the music she sang when she was young continued to be part of her nature, and she translated from time to time texts of the great German lieder which—though they cannot all be called great poetry —sang in her heart, and of which, she insisted, *singable* English versions ought to exist. These offerings to her two Muses, poetry and music, are now for the first time gathered in this book. Most of the verse from the German, for all its beauty, is marked by a melancholy acceptance of life not to be found in the passionate, occasionally protesting, often metaphysical autobiography which her *oeuvre* might be called. But it adds a chapter, so to say, to that autobiography. It also offers to American poetry-lovers an American poet's anthology of German romantic poetry unsurpassed in faithfulness to the original poems; and certain remarkable renderings of Baudelaire and of the classical French fabulist too little appreciated among us, La Fontaine.

Lewis Galantière

Acknowledgments

It is my pleasure and privilege to make the following acknowledgments:

I thank the magazine *Commentary* for first having printed in December 1957 Hermann Broch's poem, "From 'Die Schuldlosen'" with my translation now entitled "The Unnameable God."

I thank the magazine *South and West* for first publishing in their summer issue of 1962 Baudelaire's "Spleen" and Hölderlin's "Hälfte des Lebens" with my translations.

The rest of the translations in this book are now published for the first time.

I thank the following poets for their kind permission to translate their poems: Hans Sahl for "Die hölzernen Kreuze" and "Schlaflied"; Günther Anders for "Auf dem Schlachtfelde geflüstert"; Johannes Urzidil for "Manchmal sieht man längs des Badestrandes." My thanks, also, to Miriam and Naomi Beer-Hofmann for permission to translate Richard Beer-Hofmann's "Schlaflied für Mirjam" and "Lied aus 'Der junge David'"; to H. F. Broch de Rothermann and Mrs. Annemarie Meier-Graefe Broch for permission to translate "Aus 'Die Schuldlosen'"; and to Suhrkamp Verlag and Stefan Brecht for permission to translate Bertolt Brecht's "An die Nachgeborenen."

I thank H. F. Broch de Rothermann for giving me his time, his linguistic gifts and those cultural and critical qualities by reading this manuscript and making many helpful suggestions.

I thank Miriam Beer-Hofmann-Lens for procuring me the dates on my list of poets.

I thank Simon Sargon for the same service with respect to my list of composers.

Last but not least, I thank my friend and colleague, Aaron Kramer, himself poet and translator, for his generous enthusiasm and for making the first complete typescript of this collection.

Poems

Hälfte des Lebens

Mit gelben Birnen hänget
Und voll mit wilden Rosen
Das Land in den See.
Ihr holden Schwäne,
Und trunken von Küssen
Tunkt ihr das Haupt
Ins heilignüchterne Wasser.

Weh mir, wo nehm' ich wenn
Es Winter ist, die Blumen, und wo
Den Sonnenschein
Und Schatten der Erde?
Die Mauern stehn
Sprachlos und kalt, im Winde
Klirren die Fahnen.

Friedrich Hölderlin

The Half of Life

With pears of ripened yellow
And brimming with wild roses,
The land looms in the lake.
You lovely swans,
You drunken from kisses
You douse your heads
In the holy temperate water.

Ah, woe! When winter comes
Where shall I get me flowers,
Where sunshine,
And the shadows over the earth?
The walls stand
Silent and cold, in the wind
Weather vanes whirring.

Gebet für die Unheilbaren

Eil, o zaudernde Zeit, sie ans Ungereimte zu führen,
Anders belehrst du sie nie, wie verständig sie sind.

Eile, verderbe sie ganz, und führ ans fuchtbare Nichts sie,

Anders glauben sie dir nie, wie verdorben sie sind.
Diese Toren bekehren sich nie, wenn ihnen nicht schwindelt,.

Diese wandeln sich nie, wenn sie Verwesung nicht sehn.

Friedrich Hölderlin

Prayer for the Incurables

Make haste, reluctant Time, to lead them on to absurdity,
Else they will not believe nor see how they lack all under-
    standing.
Haste, undo them quite, and lead them on to the appalling
    void,
Else you will never convince them how corrupt they are.
Fools like these never reclaim themselves unless they are
    swooning,
Such do not change unless they behold the putrefaction.

Chorus Mysticus (Faust, II. Teil)

Alles Vergängliche
Ist nur ein Gleichnis;
Das Unzulängliche,
Hier wird's Ereignis;
Das Unbeschreibliche,
Hier ist's gethan;
Das Ewig-Weibliche
Zieht uns hinan.

Johann Wolfgang von Goethe

Chorus Mysticus (Faust, Part II)

Things here that pass away
All are but shadow play,
Aims past our mortal dower
There are achieved in power.
What's indescribable
There shall be known in full;
Being's eternal womb
Draws all of mankind home.

Selige Sehnsucht

Sagt es niemand, nur den Weisen,
Weil die Menge gleich verhöhnet:
Das Lebend'ge will ich preisen
Das nach Flammentod sich sehnet.

In der Liebesnächte Kühlung,
Die dich zeugte, wo du zeugtest,
Überfällt dich fremde Fühlung
Wenn die stille Kerze leuchtet.

Nicht mehr bleibest du umfangen
In der Finsternis Beschattung,
Und dich reißet neu Verlangen
Auf zu höherer Begattung.

Keine Ferne macht dich schwierig,
Kommst geflogen und gebannt,
Und zuletzt, des Lichts begierig,
Bist du Schmetterling verbrannt.

Und so lang du das nicht hast,
Dieses: Stirb und werde!
Bist du nur ein trüber Gast
Auf der dunklen Erde.

Johann Wolfgang von Goethe

Sacred Searching

Let the wise ones, only, hear it,
For the crowd derides, unthinking;
I extol the living spirit
Who the flame-death seeks, unshrinking.

In the love-nights' relaxation
Where conceived, you're now conceiving;
You are filled with rare elation
While the wicks glow, scarcely heaving.

And the shadows round you thronging
Cannot hold or keep you waiting;
You are torn anew with longing
Upward to a higher mating.

Distance ne'er to you is trying,
You come winging yet foredoomed,
Lured by light, into it flying,
Butterfly, you are consumed.

And until you learn to wrest
From each death rebirth,
You are but a dismal guest
Upon a darkling earth.

Epimenides' Erwachen (Letzte Strophe)

Verflucht sei, wer nach falschem Rat,
Mit überfrechem Mut,
Das was der Korse-Franke tat
Nun als ein Deutscher tut!

Er fühle spät, er fühle früh
Es sei ein dauernd Recht;
Ihm geh' es, trotz Gewalt und Müh,
Ihm und den Seinen schlecht!

Johann Wolfgang von Goethe

Epimenides' Awakening (Last Verse)

Accursed be he who from counsels rank
With impudent courage vies
In deed that were done by the Corsican-Frank,
And these as a German tries.

Let him feel soon, or feel it late
That Justice is reigning still,
Despite his power and plans that Fate
Bodes him and his henchmen ill!

Wanderers Nachtlied II

Über allen Gipfeln
Ist Ruh',
In allen Wipfeln
Spürest du
Kaum einen Hauch:
Die Vögelein schweigen im Walde.
Warte nur! Balde
Ruhest du auch.

Johann Wolfgang von Goethe

Wayfarer's Evensong II

Above the summits all is peace,
In all the treetops rustlings cease,
Breath-hushed in sleep.
No nestlings murmur in woods there,
Tarry now,—shortly, thou shouldst share
Slumber as deep.

Aus „Denksprüche und Merkreime"

Wär' nicht das Auge sonnenhaft,
Die Sonne könnt' es nie erblicken;
Läg' nicht in uns des Gottes eigne Kraft,
Wie könnt' uns Göttliches entzücken?

Johann Wolfgang von Goethe

Bore eye to sun no natural relation,
It could not see the sun's illumination.
And did the force divine not work in man,
How could we vibrate to the godly plan?

Das trunkene Lied

O Mensch! Gib acht!
Was spricht die tiefe Mitternacht?
„Ich schlief, ich schlief—,
Aus tiefem Traum bin ich erwacht:—
Die Welt ist tief,
Und tiefer als der Tag gedacht.
Tief ist ihr Weh—,
Lust—tiefer noch als Herzeleid:
Weh spricht: Vergeh!
Doch alle Lust will Ewigkeit—,
Will tiefe, tiefe Ewigkeit.“

Friedrich Wilhelm Nietzsche

Song of Intoxication

O Man give heed
What saith the deep midnight:
"I slept, I slept indeed,
From dream-depths waked outright.
The world is deep
And deeper than deemed by day.
Deep is its misery.
Delight hath more depth than woe:
Woe bespeaks passing away,
Delight wants eternity,
Wants all eternity, for aye."

Es genügt nicht, daß du dir kein Bild von Mir meißelst;
du denkst trotzdem in Bildern, auch wenn du Meiner ge-
denkst.
Es genügt nicht, daß du dich scheust Meinen Namen zu
nennen;
dein Denken ist Sprache, ein Nennen deine schweigende
Scheu.
Es genügt nicht, daß du an keine Götter neben Mir glaubst:
dein Glauben vermag bloß Götzen zu formen,
stellt Mich in eine Reihe mit ihnen,
wird dir bloß von ihnen anbefohlen,
nimmer von Mir.
Ich bin, und Ich bin nicht, da Ich bin. Deinem Glauben
bin Ich entrückt;
Mein Antlitz ist Nicht-Antlitz, Meine Sprache Nicht-Sprache,
und dies wußten Meine Propheten:
Anmaßung ist jegliche Aussage über Mein Sein oder Nicht-
Sein,
und die Frechheit des Leugners wie die Unterwerfung des
Gläubigen
sind gleicherweis angemaßtes Wissen;
jener flieht die Prophetenrede, und dieser mißversteht sie,

jener lehnt sich gegen Mich auf, dieser will sich Mir anbiedern
mit bequemer Verehrung,
und darum
verwerfe Ich jenen, während dieser Mein Zürnen entfacht—
eifervoll bin Ich gegen die Zutraulichen.
Ich bin der Ich nicht bin, ein brennender Dornbusch und bin
es nicht,
aber denen, welche fragen
Wen sollen wir verehren? Wer ist an unserer Spitze?
denen haben Meine Propheten geantwortet:

The Unnameable God (from "The Guiltless": Voices 1933)

It does not suffice that you hew no images of Me;
you think, nonetheless, in images, even when thinking of Me.

It does not suffice that you refrain from pronouncing My
    name;
your thinking is speech, a naming your tongue-struck timidity.

It does not suffice that you believe in no other gods than Me:
your faith, capable only of forming idols,
ranks Me with them,
and is called forth from you only by them,
never by Me.
I am and I am not in that I am. Remote am I
from your faith;
My countenance is noncountenance, My speech nonspeech,
and this was known by My prophets:
presumptuous is every declaration concerning My being or
    nonbeing,
and the insolence of the nay-sayer, like the submission of the
    faithful,
are but assumption of knowledge:
the one evades the prophets' utterance, the other conceives it
    awry,
the one revolts from Me, the other seeks to ingratiate himself
by a facile devotion.
Therefore
I cast out the one whilst the other inflames My wrath—
I am resolute against those too familiar.
I am he who I am not, a thorn bush burning, and yet I am
    not it.
But to those who ask:
Whom should we worship? and who shall be our spearhead?
to such have My prophets given answer:

Verehret! Verehret das Unbekannte, das außerhalb ist,
außerhalb eures Lagers; dort steht Mein leerer Thron
unerreichbar im leeren Nicht-Raum, in leerer Nicht-Stumm-
    heit
grenzenlos.
Schütze deine Erkenntnis!
Versuche nicht dich zu nähern. Willst du den Abstand ver-
    kleinern,
so vergrößere ihn freiwillig, und freiwillig verkrieche dich
in Zerknirschung, in die Annäherungslosigkeit deines Selbst;
dort allein bist du ebenbildhaft.
Sonst nämlich wird es dich zerknirschen. Nicht Ich werde die
Geißel über euch schwingen; ihr selber werdet sie herbei-
    holen,
und unter ihren Streichen werdet ihr eure Ebenbildhaftigkeit
verlieren, eure Erkenntnis.
Denn soferne Ich bin und soweit Ich für dich vorhanden bin,
habe Ich den Nicht-Ort Meines Wesens in dich eingesenkt,
das äußerste Außen in dein innerstes Innen—
   auf daß
   dein Erkennen zur Ahnung deines Wissens gelange,

   du aber in deinem Nicht-Glauben glauben kannst;

erkenne dein Erkennen-Können, frage dein Fragen-Können,

die Helle deiner Dunkelheit, die Dunkelheit deiner Helle,
unerhellbar, unverdunkelbar: hier ist Mein Nicht-Sein,
nirgendwo anders.
So haben es, als die Zeit reif war, Meine Propheten gelehrt,
und widerspenstig, lediglich um ihrer Auserwähltheit willen
und dennoch auserwählt, haben einige aus dem Volke
es verstanden und sich daran gehalten.
Lausche ins Unbekannte, lausche den Zeichen der neuen
    Reife,

Worship! Worship the most unknown that looms yonder,
beyond your confines; there stands My empty throne,
inaccessible in the nonspace of the void, in empty voicelessness
without boundary.
Guard well your power of perception!
Make no attempt to draw near. If you wish to lessen the dis-
    tance
then, willingly increase it, and willingly crawl
in contrition into the unapproachableness of your Self:
there alone you achieve My likeness.
Any other course means your downfall. It is not I
Who will swing the scourge upon you. You yourself will fetch it

and beneath its blows you will lose your godlikeness,
your power of perception.
For, insofar as I exist, and insofar as I am at hand for you,
have I sunk the nonlocus of My essence into you, yourself,
the uttermost outerness into your innermost recesses—
    so that
    your perceptive power may become a divination of your
        knowledge;
    you, however, in your lack of faith may yet find the gift of
        faith.
Perceive your ability to perceive, question your ability to
    question,
the light of your darkness, the darkness of your light,
unlightable, unobscurable; in this lies My nonbeing,
nowhere else.
So, when the times were ripe, have My prophets taught,
and reluctantly, simply because they had been so selected
(and, for all that, chosen), a handful of the people
heard the message and heeded it.
Hearken to the unknown, hearken to the portents of the new
    ripening,

37

daß du da seist, wenn sie anbricht für dein Erkennen. Dahin

richte deine Frömmigkeit, dein Beten. Mir jedoch gelte kein
Gebet; Ich höre es nicht: sei fromm um Meinetwillen, selbst
ohne Zugang zu Mir; das sei dein Anstand, die stolze Demut,

die dich zum Menschen macht.
Und siehe, das genügt.

Hermann Broch

that you may be there when it bursts forth for your recogni-
  tion. Toward that end
get ready with your piety and your praying. To Me, however,
address no prayer: I do not hear it; be pious for My sake, even
without access to Me. Let your bearing be one of proud
  humility
which makes you human.
And, look you, this suffices.

An die Nachgeborenen

I

Wirklich, ich lebe in finsteren Zeiten!
Das arglose Wort ist töricht. Eine glatte Stirn
Deutet auf Unempfindlichkeit hin. Der Lachende
Hat die furchtbare Nachricht
Nur noch nicht empfangen.

Was sind das für Zeiten, wo
Ein Gespräch über Bäume fast ein Verbrechen ist
Weil es ein Schweigen über so viele Untaten einschließt!
Der dort ruhig über die Straße geht
Ist wohl nicht mehr erreichbar für sein
Freunde
Die in Not sind?

Es ist wahr: ich verdiene noch meinen Unterhalt
Aber glaube mir: das ist nur ein Zufall. Nichts
Von dem, was ich tue, berechtigt mich dazu, mich sattzuessen.
Zufällig bin ich verschont. (Wenn mein Glück aussetzt
Bin ich verloren.)

Man sagt mir: Iß und trink du! Sei froh, daß du hast!
Aber wie kann ich essen und trinken, wenn
Ich dem Hungernden entreiße was ich esse, und
Mein Glas Wasser einem Verdurstenden fehlt?
Und doch esse und trinke ich.

Ich wäre gern auch weise.
In den alten Büchern steht, was weise ist:
Sich aus dem Streit der Welt halten und die kurze Zeit

Ohne Furcht verbringen
Auch ohne Gewalt auskommen
Böses mit Gutem vergelten
Seine Wünsche nicht erfüllen, sondern vergessen

To Those Born After

I

Truly I live in times of darkness!
It is foolish to speak kind words. An unruffled brow
Denotes callousness. The laugher is he
Who has not yet received the terrible news.

What sort of times are these where
A conversation about trees is almost a crime,
Because it conspires to lock so many disasters into silence;
And where he, crossing the street in tranquility,
May already be beyond the reach
Of his friends in want?

It is true: I still earn my living,
But believe me that is just accident. Nothing
That I do entitles me to eat my fill.
I am protected by chance. (If my luck departs,
I am lost.)

They say to me: Eat and drink! Be glad that you have it!
But how can I eat and drink when
I snatch what I eat from the hungry, and
The thirsty miss my glass of water.
Nevertheless, I eat and I drink.

Gladly would I, too, be wise.
It is written in the old books what wisdom consists of:
To withhold oneself from the world's strife, to pass the short
     time
Fearlessly
And to come to one's end without violence,
To repay good for evil,
Not to fulfill one's desires but to forget,

41

Gilt für weise.
Alles das kann ich nicht:
Wahrlich, ich lebe in finsteren Zeiten!

II

In die Städte kam ich zu der Zeit der Unordnung
Als da Hunger herrschte.
Unter die Menschen kam ich zu der Zeit des Aufruhrs
Und ich empörte mich mit ihnen.
So verging meine Zeit
Die auf Erden mir gegeben war.

Mein Essen aß ich zwischen den Schlachten
Schlafen legte ich mich unter die Mörder
Der Liebe pflegte ich achtlos
Und die Natur sah ich ohne Geduld.
So verging meine Zeit
Die auf Erden mir gegeben war.

Die Straßen führten in den Sumpf zu meiner Zeit.
Die Sprache verriet mich dem Schlächter.
Ich vermochte nur wenig. Aber die Herrschenden
Saßen ohne mich sicherer, das hoffte ich.
So verging meine Zeit
Die auf Erden mir gegeben war.

Die Kräfte waren gering. Das Ziel
Lag in großer Ferne,
Es war deutlich sichtbar, wenn auch für mich
Kaum zu erreichen.
So verging meine Zeit
Die auf Erden mir gegeben war.

These things suffice for wisdom.
All this can I not.
Truly I live in a time of darkness.

II

Through the cities I came in the time of disruption
Where hunger was reigning,
I came among men, I came in a time of confusion,
I joined their rebellion.
Thus passed my time,
The time bestowed upon me to spend on the earth.

I ate my food between battles
Among murderers I lay me down to sleep.
I made love perfunctorily,
I beheld nature and was impatient,
Thus passed my time,
The time bestowed upon me to spend on the earth.

The paths in my time led into a swamp.
Speech betrayed me to the slaughterer.
I prevailed but little. But the rulers
Sat more safely without me, and that was my hope.
Thus passed my time,
The time bestowed upon me to spend on the earth.

My forces were drained. The goal
Lay far in the distance.
It was plain to be seen, but as for me—
I could not attain it.
Thus passed my time,
The time bestowed upon me to spend on the earth.

43

III

Ihr, die ihr auftauchen werdet aus der Flut
In der wir untergegangen sind
Gedenkt
Wenn ihr von unseren Schwächen sprecht
Auch der finsteren Zeit
Der Ihr entronnen seid.
Gingen wir doch, öfter als die Schuhe die Länder wechselnd
Durch die Kriege der Klassen, verzweifelt
Wenn da nur Unrecht war und keine Empörung.

Dabei wissen wir ja:
Auch der Haß gegen Niedrigkeit
Verzerrt die Züge.
Auch die Zorn über das Unrecht
Macht die Stimme heiser. Ach, wir
Die wir den Boden bereiten wollten für Freundlichkeit
Konnten selber nicht freundlich sein.

Ihr aber, wenn es so weit sein wird
Daß der Mensch dem Menschen ein Helfer ist
Gedenkt unsrer
Mit Nachsicht.

Bertolt Brecht

III

You who will arise from the flood
In which we have been overwhelmed—
If our weakness be spoken of,
Remember
Also the dark times
You left behind you—
For we, who changed countries oftener than shoes,
In the wars of the classes, we went in despair
Because there was injustice but no indignation.

Withal, we knew of a certainty:
Hatred, even of meanness,
Distorts the features,
And anger, even against injustice,
Makes the voice harsh. Alas, we,
Who wished to prepare the ground for friendliness,
We ourselves could not be friendly.

But you, when it shall come to pass
That Man is the helper of men,
Think back on us
With forbearance.

Schlaflied für Mirjam

Schlaf mein Kind—schlaf, es ist spät!
Sieh wie die Sonne zur Ruhe dort geht,
Hinter den Bergen stirbt sie im Rot.
Du—du weißt nichts von Sonne und Tod,
Wendest die Augen zum Licht und zum Schein—
Schlaf, es sind soviel Sonnen noch dein,
Schlaf mein Kind—mein Kind, schlaf ein!

Schlaf mein Kind—der Abendwind weht.
Weiss man, woher er kommt, wohin er geht?
Dunkel, verborgen die Wege hier sind,
Dir, und auch mir, und uns allen, mein Kind!
Blinde—so gehn wir und gehen allein,
Keiner kann Keinem Gefährte hier sein—
Schlaf mein Kind—mein Kind, schlaf ein!

Schlaf mein Kind und horch nicht auf mich!
Sinn hats für mich nur, und Schall ists für dich.
Schall nur, wie Windeswehn, Wassergerinn,
Worte—vielleicht eines Lebens Gewinn!
Was ich gewonnen gräbt mit mir man ein,
Keiner kann Keinem ein Erbe hier sein—
Schlaf mein Kind—mein Kind, schlaf ein!

Schläfst du, Mirjam?—Mirjam, mein Kind,
Ufer nur sind wir, und tief in uns rinnt
Blut von Gewesenen—zu Kommenden rollts,
Blut unsrer Väter, voll Unruh und Stolz.
In uns sind Alle. Wer fühlt sich allein?
Du bist ihr Leben—ihr Leben ist dein—
Mirjam, mein Leben, mein Kind—schlaf ein!

Richard Beer-Hofmann

Miriam's Lullaby

Sleep, my child—sleep; it is late!
Behold the sun at the western gate,
Behind the hills, redly, yields its last breath.
But thou—thou know'st nothing of sun or of death,
Turnest thine eyes toward light and to shine—
Sleep! for so many a sun will be thine.
Sleep, my child; sleep, child of mine.

Sleep, my child—evening winds blow;
Who can say whence they come, whither they go?
Hidden the ways here and dark as a pall
For thee and for me, dear; alas, for us all.
Blindly we go and alone, I opine,
None for another the pathways untwine—
Sleep, my child; sleep, child of mine.

Sleep, child, nor hearken to me!
That which I ponder is babbling to thee,
Sounds that the wind makes or waters that run,
Words—to denote what a lifetime has won.
Me and my winnings the grave must confine;
None can another his heirship assign—
Sleep, my child; sleep, child of mine.

Art sleeping, my child? Miriam, then sleep.
We are the banks wherein currents run deep,
Blood of the past streams to future in tide,
Blood of our fathers, in turbulent pride.
Who feels alone when in him all recline?
Thou art their life, their life pulses in thine.
Miriam, my life, sleep on, child of mine.

Lied aus „Der junge David"

Schnee du, vom Hermon,
Treibt's dich zu Tale—?
Springst du ein eisiger
Quell über Stein—?

Frühling vom Berge,
Steigst du hernieder—?
Ruhst du am Hange—
Träumst du am Rain—?

Schnee du, vom Hermon,
Tränkst du die Wurzeln?
Quillt's durch dich—Ölbaum?
Schwellt es dich—Wein—?

Schnee du, vom Hermon,
Bald wirst du Traube—
Trank bald—ein Glühn unsrer
Wangen bald sein!

Richard Beer-Hofmann

Song from "The Young David"

You snow, you of Hermon,
Down drifting to valley,
On stone your pure fountain
Of ice do you break?

Is it you, Spring, I feel
On the slope as you dally
Descending the mountain
At ridge, do you dream?

You snow, you of Hermon,
Shall you water the roots soon?
Make olives moist through you?
Swell grapes by your stream?

You snow, you of Hermon,
You will be the fruit soon
The drink will be you—you
The glow on our cheek!

Manchmal sieht man längs
des Badestrandes

eine Gruppe kleiner Vögel fliegen.
Fünfe oder sechs (wie ein einheitliches Wesen)
streifen sie niedrig über der sprühenden Brandung,
nahe bei dem Getümmel der Kinder und Frauen
und der knochigen Männer, die stolz sprechen:
„Ich und das Meer!"

Aber das Vogelwesen, tief beschäftigt,
fliegt dahin, als wäre diese Küste
noch genau wie vor vielhunderttausend Jahren,
unbewohnt, unbesucht und menscheneinsam.
Die fünf oder sechs graubraunen Vögel,
die Urzeit tragen sie auf ihren kleinen Flügeln,
im Tropfennebel entschwinden sie, während droben
radargelenkte Aeroplane ihren Routen folgen
und am Horizont eine Tankerflotte vorbeischwebt.

Dann, nach einer merkwürdigen, weil nur ihr erklärlichen
     Weile,
kehrt die Gruppe der kleinen Strandvögel wieder,
mit hellen Schreien, fünfe oder sechs, wie ein Wesen.
Ihre Beute fanden sie, ihre Kriege führten sie
mit kleinem Seegetier, Krabben und Schnecken,
genau wie vor vielhunderttausend Jahren.
Siegreich entschwinden sie im zarten Perlmutterdunst,
jenseits des Getümmels der Kinder und Frauen
und der knochigen Männer, die stolz sprechen:
„Ich und das Meer!"

Johannes Urzidil

Often along the Bathing Beach One Sees

a group of small birds flying.
Five or six (like a single being) they swoop
down over the foaming surf,
near to the clamor of children and women
and the bony men, who proudly say:
"I and the sea!"

But the bird-entity, deeply engaged,
flies off, as were this coast
exactly as it was a myriad years ago,
uninhabited, unvisited, secluded from mankind.
The five or six gray-brown birds
bear primordial time on their small wings,
disappearing into the dewy fog, while above
radar-steered aeroplanes pursue their courses
and on the horizon a fleet of tankers floats past.

Then, after a peculiar interval, explicable only to them,
the group of small shore-birds returns
with shrill cries, five or six like one being.
Their booty they find, their warfare they follow
with the little creatures of the sea, crabs and snails
exactly as they did a myriad years ago.
Victorious, they vanish into the tender, nacreous mist,
beyond the clamor of children and women
and the bony men, who proudly say:
"I and the sea!"

Auf dem Schlachtfelde geflüstert
(1942: Während der deutschen Invasion Russlands)

1. Stimme:

Lieg stille, Mann. Stirb stille, Mann.
Auf unsereins kommts nimmer an.
Streck alle Viere ruhig aus,
Und denk, Du lägst im Dorf zuhaus,
Und sprächst, wie man am Sonntag spricht:
Ich bleib im Bett. Heut brauch ich nicht.

2. Stimme:

Die Sonne, Erde und der Mond
tun ihre Arbeit langgewohnt.
Auch ohne uns ist Tag und Nacht.
Auch ohne dich wird Krieg gemacht.
Von keinem Ding ist abzulesen,
Daß ich und du einst dagewesen.

3. Stimme:

Drück in den Acker dein Gesicht.
Du bist verbraucht. Dich braucht man nicht.
Noch eh' die Krume du gegessen,
bist du und ich schon längst vergessen.
Auf unsereins kommts nimmer an.
Lieg stille, Mann. Stirb stille, Mann.

Der Infantrist:

Ich weiß, die Erde und der Mond
tun ihre Arbeit langgewohnt.
Auch ohne uns wird Tag und Nacht
Und ohne uns auch Krieg gemacht.
Doch Frieden, Freiheit und Gericht,
die kommen von alleine nicht.

Whispered on the Battlefield
(1942: During the German Invasion of Russia)

1st voice:

Lie quiet, Man. Die quiet, Man.
This will never concern us again.
Stretch legs and arms upon the loam
And think you're resting there at home,
And say, as men on Sunday say:
I'll stay abed. No work today.

2nd voice:

The sun, the earth, likewise the moon,
By habit works, both late and soon.
Without us come the day and night,
And without you men wars will fight.
Nothing remains to make it clear
That one time you and I were here.

3rd voice:

Press into earth your cheek and brow.
You are all spent. None needs you now.
Quicker than crumb on which you dined
Will you and I be out of mind.
This will never concern us again.
Lie quiet, Man. Die quiet, Man.

The Infantryman:

I know the earth, likewise the moon
By habit works both late and soon.
And without us come night and day,
And wars are waged without our say.
Yet peace and law, boons of the free,
Do not, of themselves, come to be.

Die brauchen den gemeinen Mann:
Und deshalb kommt es auf uns an.

Wer immer seine Hand verloren,
Wem seine Füße abgefroren,
uns brauchen sie, die Abgehetzten,
die Rückenschüsse, Bauchverletzten.
Von jedem Stumpf sei abzulesen,
wer einmal unser Herr gewesen,
Als Warnung wollen wir sie tragen
in freieren und bessren Tagen.
Hebt aus dem Acker das Gesicht.
Man braucht euch. Rührt euch! Sterbt noch nicht!

Günther Anders

The common man upholds them all:
Therefore, through us they stand or fall.

Whoever his good hand has lost,
Or had his feet destroyed by frost,
Such need us sorely, they the hunted,
Shot in the back or bowels, stunted.
From every stump there may be read
Who was our master, held in dread,
A warning we will bear always
When freedom comes and better days.
Lift up your face from mold and wet,
You're needed. Rise. You can't die yet!

Weihnachtslied

(Vernet d'Areige, Weihnachten 1939)

Da sind wir nun alle
im Stroh, in einem Stalle
der ist nicht weniger unbequem
als der in Bethlehem.

Hier sind in engen Boxen
Esel nicht noch Ochsen,
hier ist Mäuse-und-Rattengetier
und mit ihm sind wir.

Weise vom Morgenlande
sind hier, aus jedem Stande.
Hier ist in den Herzen viel Licht;
Könige gibt es nicht.

Auch Weihrauch und Myrten
gibt es nicht. Aber Hirten
sind wir alle selbst. Unter armen Dach
sind wir sehr wach.

Weit,—Mütter verschenken
ihre Seufzer. Und könnt ihr denken
Kinder bei uns—im Regen und Schnee
hier, im Lager Vernet?

Unser Stall ist wie alle Ställe,
Unser Fall ist wie alle Fälle.
Wir haben im großen Zusammensein
das Schicksal gemein.

Hier ist eine Schlackenhalde.
Tannen stehen im Walde.
Der Wald ist vom Lager fern,
doch auch hier brennt ein Stern.

Rudolf Leonhard

Christmas Song

(Vernet d'Areige, Christmas 1939)

Now here are we all
In the straw, in a stall
Not uneasier than Him
Who lay in Bethlehem.

Here in these narrow boxes
Neither the ass nor ox is.
Here mouse and rat are free—
We keep them company.

Here wise men from the East,
The greatest and the least.
Light reigns in the heart,
No kings take part.

No incense here nor myrrh,
Yet each a shepherder
'Neath poorer roof than thatch
For himself keeps good watch.

The mothers send their sighs
As gifts.—Could they surmise
Children in snow and damp
With us in Vernet Camp?

Our stall is like all stalls,
Our fall like other falls,
Togetherness is great
That stamps a common fate.

Here is a rubbish heap.
Firs stand in forest deep.
The forest from Camp is far—
Yet here, too, burns a star.

Die hölzernen Kreuze
(Mai 1939)

Geschrieben zwischen zwei Weltkriegen

An jenem Abend, der kein Abend war,
Nur eine Pause zwischen Abfahrzeiten
Und Schlaf und Müdigkeit und Heimwärtswollen,
An jenem Abend, als du von mir gingst,
Stand ich, allein, ich weiß nicht, wie es kam,
Auf jenem Acker, der kein Acker war,
Nur Kreuze, nichts als Kreuze, irgendwo
Zwei Stunden von Paris, am Rande
Der kleinen Stadt, die keine Stadt mehr war,
Nur Tod und Schweigen und zerschossene Häuser—
Noch immer stand ich, stand und sah sie liegen,
Zehntausend Tote, die man aufgelesen
Am Morgen nach dem großen Hagelschauer,
Und schämte mich, daß ich noch stand und ging
Und atmete und liebte und mich fühlte
Und nicht mich hinwarf, wo ich hingehörte,
Dort, neben sie, bestürzt von meiner Schuld,
Noch da zu sein und lärmend, schwatzend, kauend,
Die Frist zu leben, für die jene starben.

Hans Sahl

The Wooden Crosses
(May 1939)

Written Between Two World Wars

Upon that evening that was scarcely evening,
Just a pausing between departures
And sleep, fatigue, and homeward longing,
Upon that evening as you went from me,
I stood alone, I know not how it happened,
There on that field that was a field no longer,
Just crosses, only crosses, lying somewhere
Two hours away from Paris on the outskirts
Of a town that was a town no longer,
Just death and silence and demolished houses—
I kept on standing, stood and saw them lying
Ten thousand dead who had been gleaned there
The morning after death's great hailstorm,
And was ashamed that I could stand or go
And breathe and love and be thus self-aware
And still not cast myself where I belonged
There, next to them, perplexed at my own fault
In being there, and clamoring, chattering, munching
The grant of life for which these dead had died.

Schlaflied

Höre auf zu beweinen,
Gib der Eitelkeit Ruh',
Immer findest du einen,
Der mächtiger ist als du.

Klage nicht, bleibe am Leben,
Frage nicht mehr: wozu?
Immer wird's einen geben,
Der hungriger ist als du.

Hans Sahl

Lullaby

Cease now your bewailing,
And vanity subdue,
You will always find another
Who is mightier than you.

Lament not; keep on living,
Nor ask: what will ensue?
You will always find another
Who is hungrier than you.

Ade, nun, zur guten Nacht

Ade, nun, zur guten Nacht.
Nun wird der Schluß gemacht,
Daß ich muß scheiden.
Im Winter, da schneit der Schnee,
Im Sommer, da blüht der Klee,
Dann kehr ich wieder.

Volkslied

Good-bye Now and Good Night

Good-bye now and good night.
The end is now in sight,
For we must part in twain.
In winter there come the snows,
In summer the clover blows,
And then I'll come again.

Folksong

Aus „Galgenlieder"

Der Lattenzaun

Es war einmal ein Lattenzaun,
mit Zwischenraum, hindurchzuschaun.

Ein Architekt, der dieses sah,
stand eines Abends plötzlich da—

und nahm den Zwischenraum heraus
und baute draus ein großes Haus.

Der Zaun indessen stand ganz dumm,
mit Latten ohne was herum.

ein Anblick gräßlich und gemein.
Drum zog ihn der Senat auch ein.

Der Architekt jedoch entfloh
nach Afri—od—Ameriko.

Christian Morgenstern

The Picket Fence

A picket fence once came to view
With interspaces one looked through.

An architect who this espied
Came suddenly one evening; pried

The interspaces out, ahem!
A fine large house he built of them.

Meanwhile the fence stood there astounded!
Its pickets bare, with naught around it,

A sight provoking dread offense,
The senate moved the thing from thence.

The architect departed, though,
For Afri—or—Americo.

Der Seufzer

Ein Seufzer lief Schlittschuh auf nächtlichem Eis
    und träumte von Liebe und Freude.
Es war an dem Stadtwall, und schneeweiß
    glänzten die Stadtwallgebäude.

Der Seufzer dacht' an ein Maidelein
    und blieb erglühend stehen.
Da schmolz die Eisbahn unter ihm ein—
    und er sank—und ward nimmer gesehen.

Christian Morgenstern

The Sigh

On skates through the darkness a sigh braved the ice,
  Of love and of joy fell a-dreaming,
'Twas there on the bastion where each edifice
  White in the snowshine was gleaming.

Then mused the sigh on a maiden fair,
  Standing still with his heart in a glow.
Beneath him the rink melted into thin air—
  And he sank—and was seen nevermo'.

Der Purzelbaum

Ein Purzelbaum trat vor mich hin
und sagte: „Du nur siehst mich
und weißt, was für ein Baum ich bin:
Ich schieße nicht, man schießt mich.

Und trag' ich Frucht? Ich glaube kaum;
auch bin ich nicht verwurzelt.
Ich bin nur noch ein Purzeltraum,
sobald ich hingepurzelt.“

Jenun, so sprach ich, „Bester Schatz,
du bist doch klug und siehst uns;—
nun, auch für uns besteht der Satz:
Wir schießen nicht, es schießt uns.

Auch Wurzeln treibt man nicht so bald
und Früchte nun erst recht nicht.
Geh heim in deinen Purzelwald
and lästre dein Geschlecht nicht.“

Christian Morgenstern

The Somersault

A somersault, the Germans name
A tumble-tree, addressed me thus:
"You know trees of the kind such as I am
Can't throw themselves, something throws us.

To call what I bear 'fruit,' I'd spurn,
Nor have I any roots 'twould seem:
As soon as I have done my turn
I turn into a tumble-dream."

Then I: "Wise friend, most dear to me,
Your dictum could of us be stated,
We don't ejaculate, you see;
Instead we are ejaculated.

We do not bear the fruit we should,
Our claim to roots is a pretender;
Go back into your tumble-wood,
And nevermore abuse your gender."

Das Knie

Ein Knie geht einsam durch die Welt.
Es ist ein Knie, sonst nichts!
Es ist kein Baum! Es ist kein Zelt!
Es ist ein Knie, sonst nichts.

Im Kriege ward einmal ein Mann
erschossen um und um.
Das Knie allein blieb unverletzt—
als wär's ein Heiligtum.

Seitdem geht's einsam durch die Welt.
Es ist ein Knie, sonst nichts.
Es ist kein Baum, es ist kein Zelt.
Es ist ein Knie, sonst nichts.

Christian Morgenstern

The Knee

Goes lonely through the world a knee.
It is a knee, naught else!
It is no tent! It is no tree!
It is a knee, naught else.

Once in the war a man unarmed
Was riddled from every side.
Only the knee remained unharmed—
As relics oft betide.

Since then, lone wanderer, the knee.
It is a knee, naught else.
It is no tent, it is no tree.
It is a knee, naught else.

Berufung (1913)

„Steh auf! Die Zeit soll ihren Seher finden!“
Weiß stand ein Engel in dem Dämmergrau.
Ich schrak zurück: „Verschone du mich Blinden!“
Der Engel küßte mir die Augen: „Schau!“

Und sieh’, da wuchs ein riesenhafter Bau
Auf aus dem Dunste mit traumhafter Jähe,
Verschwamm hoch oben mit des Himmels Blau.
Der Engel küßte mir die Füße: „Gehe!“

Ich stieg empor bis in des Himmels Nähe
Vieltausend Stufen . . . „Herr, was soll hier ich?“—
„Ruf’ einmal Gnade und ruf’ dreimal Wehe!
Den Himmel über dir, schau unter dich!“

Ich sah hinab und Grausen faßte mich . . .
Der Engel küßte mir die Lippen: „Sprich!“

Uriel Birnbaum

The Call (1913)

"Arise! The age its seer has need to find!"
White stood an angel in the dusky nook.
I shuddered back. "Shield me, lest I go blind."
The angel kissed me on the eyes with, "Look!"

Behold! Gigantically, there came to view
A structure, with the suddenness dreams show,
And rose through mist and merged with heaven's blue.
The angel kissed my feet and murmured: "Go!"

I mounted many thousand steps till, lo!
I neared the heavens. "Lord, why am I here?"
"Call up the blessing once, thrice call down woe.
With heaven above you, now beneath you peer."

I looked below and panic made me weak.
The angel kissed my lips and whispered: "Speak!"

תְּפִלַּת אִשָּׁה

שָׁמְרֵנִי, אֱלֹהִים, מֵרוּחַ קָרָה
וּמֵרוּחַ שׂוֹרֶפֶת
לְמַעַן שְׁלוֹם הַלּוּל וְהַגִּנָּה וְהַפְּרָה
שֶׁבָּרֶפֶת.

וְגַם בַּעֲבוּר שֶׁלְּקַחְתַּנִי, עֲנֻגָּה מֵרֶחֶם,
מֵאָב זָקֵן וּמֵאֵם זְקֵנָה
לְהוֹצִיא מִקַּרְקַע סְגוּפָה לֶחֶם
וְגַם תְּאֵנָה.

וּבַעֲבוּר שֶׁקִּבַּלְתִּי עָלַי בְּאַהֲבָה וּבְדְמָמָה
כָּל הַטּוֹב וְהָרָע;
אֲשֶׁר גּוֹעָה הַבְּהֵמָה וּנְמוּכָה הַקָּמָה
וַאֲנִי גַם הָרָה.

Judah Karni

Since it is well-nigh impossible to get the Hebrew text
above put into a phonetic version on which scholars agree,
I am printing it as it was originally published. I do not
read Hebrew. In 1952, inspired by Dr. Simon Halkin's book,
Modern Hebrew Writers, I became eager to learn more. In
answer to letters requesting help, Dr. Simon Halkin and
Dr. Gershon Scholem, both professors at the Hebrew Uni-
versity of Jerusalem, sent me English-speaking scholars to
lighten my labors. Dr. Gabriel Preil and Baruch Hochman
came often to my home and gave me generously of their
knowledge and enthusiasm. With the aid of their literal

Prayer of a Woman

God, keep me from the blast that's raw,
And from the burning blast;
For the sake of the garden, the fledgling's maw,
And the cow in the stall made fast.

For me, who was pampered from my birth,
You took from old Mother and Father,
To wrest my bread from afflicted earth,
From the desert-palm dates to gather.

In love and silence I took on
My fate, both harsh and mild;
So help me, for the corn's not grown,
The beast lows, I'm with child.

translations I tried my hand at English versions of Israeli
poetry.

It was young Hochman who first read to me Judah
Karni's "Prayer of a Woman." He read and reread it until
I absorbed its music and meaning, and on the spot wrote
my translation. The poem became mine. I was that woman,
a thousand years ago, a thousand years in the future, or
today in Israel on a kibbutz. This sense of identification
was not a slight madness. When I sent a copy of my transla-
tion to my friend Sylvia Townsend Warner, she wrote to
me, "It sounds so much like you, you could have written it
yourself."

J'ai plus de souvenirs que si j'avais mille ans.

Un gros meuble à tiroirs encombré de bilans,
De vers, de billets doux, de procès, de romances,
Avec de lourds cheveux roulés dans des quittances,
Cache moins de secrets que mon triste cerveau.
C'est une pyramide, un immense caveau,
Que contient plus de morts que la fosse commune.
—Je suis un cimetière abhorré de la lune,
Où, comme des remords, se traînent de longs vers
Qui s'acharnent toujours sur mes morts les plus chers.
Je suis un vieux boudoir plein de roses fanées,
Où gît tout un fouillis de modes surannées,
Où les pastels plaintifs et les pâles Boucher,
Seuls, respirent l'odeur d'un flacon débouché.
Rien n'égale en longueur les boiteuses journées,
Quand sous les lourds flocons des neigeuses années
L'ennui, fruit de la morne incuriosité,
Prend les proportions de l'immortalité.
—Désormais tu n'es plus, ô matière vivante!
Qu'un granit entouré d'une vague épouvante,
Assoupi dans le fond d'un Sahara brumeux!
Un vieux sphinx ignoré du monde insoucieux,
Oublié sur la carte, et dont l'humeur farouche
Ne chante qu'aux rayons du soleil qui se couche.

Charles Baudelaire

Spleen II

Keepsakes!—I might have lived a thousand years!—

A chest of drawers, large, littered with arrears,
With verses, love-notes, novels, writs replete,
And many a tress wrapped in an old receipt,
Stores fewer secrets than—downcast and dense—
My brain: a pyramid, a cave immense,
Hoarding more dead than does the potter's field.
—I am a graveyard whence the moon has fled,
Where, like remorse, worms drag and will not yield
From battening ever on my cherished dead.
I am an old boudoir full of wan roses,
Where scattered clothing, long passé, reposes,
Where pallid Bouchers and where sad pastels
Alone breathe in from opened flasks their smells.
Unmatched, the tedium of these days that go
Sagging beneath massed flakes from years of snow,
When boredom, fruit of witless apathy,
Takes on dimensions of eternity.
—O living matter, thou art now no more
Than thing of granite, dormant on the floor
Of dim Sahara, circled by vague horror;
An old sphinx which the heedless world forgets,
Neglected on the map, whose surly humor
Sings to the sun rays only when sun sets.

Un philosophe austère, et né dans la Scythie,
Se proposant de suivre une plus douce vie,
Voyagea chez les Grecs, et vit en certains lieux
Un sage assez semblable au vieillard de Virgile,
Homme égalant les rois, homme approchant des dieux,
Et, comme ces derniers, satisfait et tranquille.
Son bonheur consistait aux beautés d'un jardin.
Le Scythe l'y trouva, qui la serpe à la main,
De ses arbres à fruits retranchait l'inutile,
Ébranchait, émondait, ôtait ceci, cela,
    Corrigeant partout la nature,
Excessive à payer ses soins avec usure.
    Le Scythe alors lui demanda
Pourquoi cette ruine. Était-il d'homme sage
De mutiler ainsi ces pauvres habitants?
"Quittez-moi votre serpe, instrument de dommage;
    Laissez agir la faux du temps:
Ils iront assez tôt border le noir rivage."
"—J'ôte le superflu, dit l'autre, et l'abattant,
    Le reste en profite d'autant."
Le Scythe, retourné dans sa triste demeure,
Prend la serpe à son tour, coupe et taille à toute heure;
Conseille à ses voisins, prescrit à ses amis
    Un universel abatis.
Il ôte de chez lui les branches les plus belles,
Il tronque son verger contre toute raison,
    Sans observer temps ni saison,
    Lunes ni vieilles ni nouvelles.
Tout languit et tout meurt. Ce Scythe exprime bien
    Un indiscret stoïcien.
    Celui-ci retranche de l'âme
Désirs et passions, le bon et le mauvais,
    Jusqu'aux plus innocents souhaits.

The Scythian Philosopher (XII, 20)

A Scythian philosopher, austere,
Abandoned Scythia for Greece because
He planned to mold his life by milder laws;
And once on soil to noble Plato dear
He met a man like that one Virgil praised,
A wizard, kinglike, godlike, who amazed
Because, like gods, he was content, serene,
Finding his joy within his garden, green.
And there was found, his pruning hook in hand,
Thinning his fruit trees with demeanor bland,
Scraping a bole or lopping off a limb,
Now here, now there, to make all nature trim.
She in return repaid with interest
The ardor for her welfare thus expressed.
The Scythian now asked him in surprise
"Why, pray, this ruin? Do you think it wise
To mutilate your inoffensive trees?
Give me your pruning hook, relinquish these
To Time, who'll add all to his rubbish store,
And cast it soon on that dark river's shore."
The sage replied: "I only cut away
Dead wood and shoots that hinder the life spray."
The Scythian went home to his bleak house,
Took up his pruning hook, went at his boughs
Like one possessed and, contrary to reason,
Through weary hours, in and out of season,
Whether the moon was on the wane or new,
And bade his friends and neighbors do so too.
He hacked away until all failed and died.
The Scythian provides a paradigm
Of foolish Stoics, who behaved like him,
Who, in their efforts for the soul, have tried
To stamp out every passion and desire,

Contre de telles gens, quant à moi, je réclame.
Ils ôtent à nos coeurs le principal ressort:
Ils font cesser de vivre avant que l'on soit mort.

Jean de La Fontaine

Both good and bad; to keep their code entire,
Ruled out our joys to the most innocent.
But, for my part, such people I resent,
Who from our hearts the main support would shear,
Making life cease long before death draws near.

L'Écolier, le Pédant, et le Maître d'un Jardin (IX, 5)

Certain enfant qui sentait son collège,
Doublement sot, et doublement fripon,
Par le jeune âge, et par le privilège
Qu'ont les pédants de gâter la raison,
Chez un voisin dérobait, ce dit-on,
Et fleurs et fruits. Ce voisin, en automne,
Des plus beaux dons que nous offre Pomone
Avait la fleur, les autres le rebut.
Chaque saison apportait son tribut.
Car au printemps il jouissait encore
Des plus beaux dons que nous présente Flore.
Un jour dans son jardin il vit notre écolier,
Qui grimpant sans égard sur un arbre fruitier,
Gâtait jusqu'aux boutons, douce et frêle espérance,
Avant-coureurs des biens que promet l'abondance.
Même il ébranchait l'arbre, et fit tant à la fin
Que le possesseur du jardin
Envoya faire plainte au maître de la classe.
Celui-ci vint suivi d'un cortège d'enfants.
Voilà le verger plein de gens
Pires que le premier. Le pédant, de sa grâce,
Accrut le mal en amenant
Cette jeunesse mal instruite :
Le tout, à ce qu'il dit, pour faire un châtiment
Qui pût servir d'exemple, et dont toute sa suite
Se souvînt à jamais comme d'une leçon.
Là-dessus il cita Virgile et Cicéron,
Avec force traits de science.
Son discours dura tant que la maudite engeance
Eut le temps de gâter en cent lieux le jardin.
Je hais les pièces d'éloquence
Hors de leur place et qui n'ont point de fin,
Et ne sais bête au monde pire

The Schoolboy, the Pedant, and the Man with a Garden (IX, 5)

A certain boy, who typifies his school,
Dull-witted and of deviltry too full,
Because, in the first place, of unripe age,
In second place, because the privilege
Of pedants is to stultify the sense,
Crossed flagrantly, 'tis said, his neighbor's fence
And robbed the good man of his fruit and flowers,
Creating stormlike havoc in those bowers
Which gave, in autumn, reason to rejoice,
For then Pomona yielded him the choice
Of her ripe gifts—to others the leftovers;
Each turn of year was the return of favors:
For Spring was less a season and far more a
Brief grant of paradise bestowed by Flora.
One day this landlord saw within his close
Our schoolboy, who, without compunction, chose
To clamber up a frail and flowering tree,
Shake down its promising buds and, finally,
What with its broken limbs and broken hopes
Of future bearing gave such cause for mopes
That, having no defense against disaster,
The landlord sent his plaint to the schoolmaster,
Who came with escort of his hobbledehoys,
All, like the culprit, uncouth, ill-trained boys,
And wreaking all more damage than the first.
The pedant—of all bores the most accursed—
Declared that his intention was to show
(By quoting Virgil, yes, and Cicero,
Propped up by exegeses without end)
How one chastisement would serve both to bend
The evil-doer's will and likewise lend
Example that would future wrack forfend.
I hate these flights of windy eloquence,

Que l'écolier, si ce n'est le pédant.
Le meilleur de ces deux pour voisin, à vrai dire,
    Ne me plairait aucunement.

Jean de La Fontaine

Misplaced and dragged through periods beyond number:
If there be creatures that this earth encumber
Worse than the schoolboy, 'tis the teacher-dunce.
Choose which for neighbor? Faith, to answer true
Either would be the source of endless rue.

Phébus et Borée (VI, 3)

Borée et le Soleil virent un voyageur
   Qui s'était muni par bonheur
Contre le mauvais temps. On entrait dans l'automne,
Quand la précaution aux voyageurs est bonne:
Il pleut; le soleil luit; et l'écharpe d'Iris
   Rend ceux qui sortent avertis
Qu'en ces mois le manteau leur est fort nécessaire.
Les Latins les nommaient douteux pour cette affaire.
Notre homme s'était donc à la pluie attendu:
Bon manteau bien doublé; bonne étoffe bien forte.
"Celui-ci, dit le vent, prétend avoir pourvu
À tous les accidents; mais il n'a pas prévu
   Que je saurai souffler de sorte
Qu'il n'est bouton qui tienne: il faudra, si je veux,
   Que le manteau s'en aille au diable.
L'ébattement pourrait nous en être agréable:
Vous plaît-il de l'avoir? —Eh bien, gageons nous deux,
   Dit Phébus, sans tant de paroles,
À qui plutôt aura dégarni les épaules
   Du cavalier que nous voyons.
Commencez. Je vous laisse obscurcir mes rayons."
Il n'en fallut pas plus. Notre souffleur à gage
Se gorge de vapeurs, s'enfle comme un ballon,
   Fait un vacarme de démon,
Siffle, souffle, tempête, et brise en son passage
Maint toit quit n'en peut mais, fait périr maint bateau;
   Le tout au sujet d'un manteau.
Le cavalier eut soin d'empêcher que l'orage
   Ne se pût engouffrer dedans.
Cela le préserva; le vent perdit son temps:
Plus il se tourmentait, plus l'autre tenait ferme;
Il eut beau faire agir le collet et les plis.
   Sitôt qu'il fut au bout du terme
   Qu'à la gageure on avait mis,
   Le soleil dissipe la nue,
Récrée, et puis pénètre enfin le cavalier,

Phoebus and Boreas (VI, 3)

The north wind and the sun one day espied
A traveler set out, well fortified
Against bad weather. It was in the fall,
When to foresee is largely to forestall
The hazards of the rain and sun and change:
So prudent are the folk who plan to range
To be equipped for every circumstance
In months on which the Latins look askance.
Our man was ready. Let the rain be rough,
His cloak was lined and of a good stout stuff.
"This fellow," said the wind, "meant to prepare
For all contingencies, though unaware
That when I want I know to raise a blast
That not a button on his cloak holds fast.
A button? Without boasting I can say
His whole coat straight to hell I'll blow away.
This may provide diversion for us yet.
What do you say, old Sol?" "Let's make a bet,"
Replied the sun, "and without more ado,
'Twill be a trial of strength between us two
To see if you or I the sooner bares
The shoulders of this gallant as he fares.
Start off at once! You may call up a cloud."
So said, so done. Our better puffs aloud,
Fills up on wind, swells like a great balloon,
Accelerates a breeze to a typhoon,
Howls like a demon, and—put to the proof—
Blows, whistles, storms, as he rips off a roof
From many a house and founders many a boat.
And all this bluster to undo a coat.
The gallant, meanwhile, took care to prevent
Wind's inward sally through a seam or rent.
This is what saved him. Wind it was who lost.
The traveler stood firm, though at a cost
Of effort to hold fast at neck and skirt.
The betting time was up and now, alert,

Sous son balandras fait qu'il sue,
Le contraint de s'en dépouiller.
Encore n'usa-t-il pas de toute sa puissance.
Plus fait douceur que violence.

Jean de La Fontaine

The sun dispersed the cloud and then he turned
Reviving rays upon our man and burned
Right through his cape till, sweating hard, he tore
And cast aside the garment that he wore.
The sun did this with less force than the gale's.
So mildness often wins where fury fails.

Verses Set to Music

Der Asra

Täglich ging die wunderschöne
Sultanstochter auf und nieder
Um die Abendzeit am Springbrunn,
Wo die weißen Wasser plätschern.

Täglich stand der junge Sklave
Um die Abendzeit am Springbrunn,
Wo die weißen Wasser plätschern;
Täglich ward er bleich und bleicher.

Eines Abends trat die Fürstin
Auf ihn zu mit raschen Worten:
„Deinen Namen will ich wissen,
Deine Heimat, deine Sippschaft!"

Und der Sklave sprach: „Ich heiße
Mohamet, ich bin aus Jemen,
Und mein Stamm sind jene Asra,
Welche sterben, wenn sie lieben."

Heinrich Heine
(*Anton Rubinstein*)

The Azra

Every day the wondrous lovely
Sultan's daughter came there strolling
In the evening near the fountain
Where the foaming water plashes.

Every day there stood the slave boy
In the evening near the fountain
Where the foaming water plashes . . .
Daily he grew pale and paler.

Then one evening came the princess
To his side with hurried phrases:
"Tell your name, for I would know it:
Where your country, who your kindred!"

And the slave replied: "My name is
Mohamet, I come from Yemen.
And my tribesmen are those Azra,
Who when loving have to perish."

Der Schmied

Ich hör' meinen Schatz
Den Hammer er schwinget,
Das rauschet, das klinget,
Das dringt in die Weite
Wie Glockengeläute
Durch Gassen und Platz.

Am schwarzen Kamin,
Da sitzet mein Lieber,
Doch geh' ich vorüber,
Die Bälge dann sausen,
Die Flammen aufbrausen
Und lodern um ihn.

Ludwig Uhland
(*Johannes Brahms*)

The Smith

My sweetheart I hear,
He's swinging his hammer,
The clinking, the clamor
Resound in far places,
Like bell-peals whose traces
Reach alleys and square.

Before the black forge
My lover is sitting,
When I go past, flitting,
The bellows are roaring,
The flames higher soaring
Around him they surge.

Wie komm' ich denn zur Tür herein

„Wie komm' ich denn zur Tür herein
Sag' du, mein Liebchen, sag'
Wie komm' ich denn zur Tür herein
Sag' du, mein Liebchen, sag'."

„Nimm den Ring und zieh' die Klink
Dann meint die Mutter es wär' der Wind.
O komm', mein Liebchen, komm'
Komm' du mein Liebchen, komm'."

„Wie komm' ich denn vorbei dem Feu'r,
Sag' du, mein Liebchen, sag'—
Wie komm' ich denn vorbei dem Feu'r,
Sag' du, mein Liebchen, sag'."

„Schütt' ein bischen Wasser d'rein,
Dann meint die Mutter es regnet rein.
Komm' du, mein Liebchen, komm',
O komm', mein Liebchen, komm'."

„Wie komm' ich denn vorbei dem Hund,
Sag' du, mein Liebchen, sag',
Wie komm' ich denn vorbei dem Hund,
Sag' du, mein Liebchen, sag'."

„Gib dem Hund ein gutes Wort
Dann geht er wieder an seinen Ort,
Komm' du, mein Liebchen, komm',
O komm', mein Liebchen, komm'."

„Wie komm' ich denn die Trepp' hinauf
Sag' du, mein Liebchen, sag',
Wie komm' ich denn die Trepp' hinauf
Sag' du, mein Liebchen, sag'."

How Shall I Get Inside the Door

How shall I get inside the door,
Tell me, my darling, do.
How shall I get inside the door,
Tell me, my darling, do.

Grasp the ring and pull the lock
And mother'll think the wind makes mock—
Oh, come, my darling, come;
Come, come, my darling, come.

How shall I pass before the fire,
Tell me, my darling, do.
How shall I pass before the fire,
Tell me, my darling, do.

Douse the flame with droplets thin
And mother'll think it's raining in.
Oh, come, my darling, come;
Come, come, my darling, come.

How shall I get me past the dog,
Tell me, my darling, do.
How shall I get me past the dog,
Tell me, my darling, do.

Speak a kindly word to Trace
And he'll go back into his place . . .
Oh, come, my darling, come;
Come, come, my darling, come.

But how shall I get up the stairs,
Tell me, my darling, do.
But how shall I get up the stairs,
Tell me, my darling, do.

„Nimm die Schuh' nur in die Hand
Und schleich dich leis' entlang der Wand.
Komm' du, mein Liebchen, komm'.
Komm', komm', mein Liebchen, komm'!"

Volkslied
(*Johannes Brahms*)

Take your shoes in hand, that's all,
And softly glide along the wall.
Come, come, my darling, come;
Come, come, my darling, come!

Folksong

Mädchenlied

Auf die Nacht in der Spinnstub'n,
Da singen die Mädchen,
Da lachen die Dorfbub'n,
Wie flink geh'n die Rädchen!

Spinnt Jedes am Brautschatz,
Daß der Liebste sich freut.
Nicht lange, so gibt es
Ein Hochzeitgeläut.

Kein Mensch, der mir gut ist,
Will nach mir fragen;
Wie bang mir zu Muth ist,
Wem soll ich's klagen?

Die Thränen rinnen
Mir über's Gesicht—
Wofür soll ich spinnen?
Ich weiß es nicht!

Paul Heyse
(*Johannes Brahms*)

Maiden's Song

In the workroom the maidens
Sing as nightfall comes blurring,
The town lads lounge laughing,
The spindles are whirring.

Each one spins for her dowry
That her sweetheart rejoice;
Not far off 'twould seem now
A wedding's glad noise.

Not a soul who is kindly
Asks how I'm faring,
How anxious my heart is,
Its plaint no one sharing.

Adown my features
The tears start to flow.
Then why go on spinning?
I do not know.

Salamander

Es saß ein Salamander
Auf einem kühlen Stein,
Da warf ein böses Mädchen
In's Feuer ihn hinein.

Sie meint, er soll verbrennen,
Ihm ward erst wohl zu Mut,
Wohl wie wir kühlem Teufel
Die heiße Liebe tut.

Karl von Lemcke
(Johannes Brahms)

The Salamander

A salamander resting
Upon a chilly stone
Was by a wicked maiden
Into the fire thrown.

She thought it would consume him;
Now in his element,
Like us cool-hearted devils
Who hot love makes content.

Denk' es, o Seele!

Ein Tännlein grünet wo,
Wer weiß, im Walde,
Ein Rosenstrauch, wer sagt,
In welchem Garten?
Sie sind erlesen schon—
Denk' es, o Seele!—
Auf deinem Grab zu wurzeln
Und zu wachsen.

Zwei schwarze Rößlein weiden
Auf der Wiese,
Sie kehren heim zur Stadt
In muntern Sprüngen.
Sie werden schrittweis gehn
Mit deiner Leiche,
Vielleicht, vielleicht noch eh'
An ihren Hufen
Das Eisen los wird,
Das ich blitzen seh'.

Eduard Mörike
(*Hugo Wolf*)

My Soul, Consider!

Somewhere a fir shoot sprouts,
Who knows in what forest?
A rosebush thrives,
Who'll say in which garden?
They're destined even now—
My soul, consider!—
On thy grave to be planted,
There to flourish.

Two bright black colts
Are browsing on the meadow,
They canter home to town
With gay cavortings
They'll draw slow step by step
Thy lifeless body,
Perhaps—perhaps—before,
Off from their frisking hooves,
The iron shoes fall,
That I now see, glinting.

Verborgenheit

Laß, o Welt, o laß mich sein!
Locket nicht mit Liebesgaben,
Laßt dies Herz alleine haben
Seine Wonne, seine Pein!

Was ich traure weiß ich nicht,
Es ist unbekanntes Wehe;
Immerdar durch Tränen sehe
Ich der Sonne liebes Licht.

Oft bin ich mir kaum bewußt,
Und die helle Freude zücket
Durch die Schwere, so mich drücket
Wonniglich in meiner Brust.

Laß, o Welt, o laß mich sein!
Locket nicht mit Liebesgaben,
Laßt dies Herz alleine haben
Seine Wonne, seine Pein!

Eduard Mörike
(Hugo Wolf)

Seclusion

World, o let me thus remain,
Lure me not with love's sweet favor,
Let this heart in loneness savor
Its own rapture and its pain.

I mourn yet know not aright
What to call this latent anguish,
Through my tears, the while I languish,
I can see the sun's dear light.

Often when I'm sore depressed,
Almost unaware, the healing—
Joy transcendent—enters, stealing
Blissfully into my breast.

World, o let me thus remain,
Lure me not with love's sweet favor,
Let this heart in loneness savor
Its own rapture and its pain.

Gesang Weylas

Du bist Orplid, mein Land!
Das ferne leuchtet;
Vom Meere dampfet dein besonnter Strand
Den Nebel, so der Götter Wange feuchtet.

Uralte Wasser steigen
Verjüngt um deine Hüften, Kind!
Vor deiner Gottheit beugen
Sich Könige, die deine Wärter sind.

Eduard Mörike
(Hugo Wolf)

Weyla's Song

Orplid, my far-off land,
Thy radiance streaming!
From ocean's merging with thy sunny strand
Rise vapors, moistly on the god's cheeks gleaming.

Primordial waters rise and flow
About thy flanks, renewed there. Child!
Before thy godhead kings shall bow
As vassals pledged unto thy service mild.

Das verlassene Mägdlein

Früh, wann die Hähne krähn,
Eh' die Sternlein schwinden,
Muß ich am Herde stehn,
Muß Feuer zünden.

Schön ist der Flammen Schein,
Es springen die Funken;
Ich schaue so darein,
In Leid versunken.

Plötzlich, da kommt es mir,
Treuloser Knabe,
Daß ich die Nacht von dir
Geträumet habe.

Träne auf Träne dann
Stürzet hernieder,
So kommt der Tag heran—
O ging' er wieder!

Eduard Mörike
(Hugo Wolf)

The Maid Forsaken

Early, when cocks do crow,
E'er the stars expire,
To the hearth I must go,
Must light the fire.

Lovely the shining blaze,
Sparks flying like arrows,
Blankly therein I gaze,
Sunk in my sorrows.

Swiftly a thought breaks through,
Oh, faithless lover!
Last night I dreamed of you,
Over and over.

Tear after stumbling tear
Falls down untended;
So does the day appear—
Oh, were it ended!

Auch kleine Dinge

Auch kleine Dinge
Können uns entzücken,
Auch kleine Dinge
Können teuer sein.

Bedenkt, wie gern
Wir uns mit Perlen schmücken,
Sie sind so klein
Und doch so schwer bezahlt.

Bedenkt, wie klein
Ist die Olivenfrucht,
Und wird um ihre Güte
Doch gesucht.

Denkt an die Rose nur,
Wie klein sie ist,
Und duftet doch so lieblich,
Wie ihr wißt.

Paul Heyse
(Hugo Wolf)

Aye, Even Small Things

Aye, even small things
Have the power to charm us,
Aye, even small things
Can be treasure-fraught.

Reflect, how fain
We seek pearls to adorn us.
They are so small
And yet so dearly bought.

How small the fruit
The silver olives bear,
Yet for its savor
Sought everywhere.

Muse on the rose alone,
How small it is,
Yet wafts such lovely fragrance—
Well you know this.

Gretchen am Spinnrade

Meine Ruh' ist hin,
Mein Herz ist schwer;
Ich finde, ich finde
Sie nimmer und nimmermehr.

Wo ich ihn nicht hab'
Ist mir das Grab,
Die ganze Welt
Ist mir vergällt.

Mein armer Kopf
Ist mir verrückt,
Mein armer Sinn
Ist mir zerstückt.

Meine Ruh' ist hin,
Mein Herz ist schwer;
Ich finde, ich finde
Sie nimmer und nimmermehr.

Nach ihn nur schau' ich
Zum Fenster hinaus,
Nach ihn nur geh' ich
Aus dem Haus.

Sein hoher Gang,
Sein' edle Gestalt,
Seines Mundes Lächeln,
Seiner Augen Gewalt,

Und seiner Rede,
Zauberfluß!
Sein Händedruck,
Und ach! sein Kuß!

Margaret at the Spinning Wheel

My peace is gone,
My heart is sore,
My peace, I shall find it never,
Oh, nevermore.

Where he cannot be,
The grave is to me,
The world and all
Is tinged with gall.

My poor, poor head
Is turned awry,
My poor, poor wits
To tatters fly.

My peace is gone,
My heart is sore,
My peace, I shall find it never,
Oh, nevermore.

To watch him only
I peer through the pane,
I leave the house only
To see him again.

His stately tread,
His noble build,
His mouth when smiling,
His eyes, power-filled,

His flowing discourse,
Magic, it is!
His hand on one,
And, ah! his kiss!

Meine Ruh' ist hin,
Mein Herz ist schwer;
Ich finde, ich finde
Sie nimmer und nimmermehr.

Mein Busen drängt sich
Nach ihm hin.
Ach, dürft' ich ihn fassen
Und halten ihn!

Und küssen ihn,
So wie ich wollt',
An seinen Küssen
Vergehen sollt'!

Meine Ruh' ist hin,
Mein Herz ist schwer.

Johann Wolfgang von Goethe
(Franz Schubert)

My peace is gone,
My heart is sore,
My peace, I shall find it never,
Oh, nevermore.

My heart pursues him
When he has passed,
Oh, might I embrace him
And hold him fast,

And kiss him as
None can but I,
Upon his kisses
Be let to die!

My peace is gone,
My heart is sore.

Die Krähe

Eine Krähe war mit mir
Aus der Stadt gezogen,
Ist bis heute für und für
Um mein Haupt geflogen.

Krähe, wunderliches Tier,
Willst mich nicht verlassen?
Meinst wohl bald als Beute hier
Meinen Leib zu fassen?

Nun, es wird nicht weit mehr geh'n
An dem Wanderstabe;
Krähe, lass' mich endlich seh'n
Treue bis zum Grabe.

Wilhelm Müller
(Franz Schubert)

The Crow

From the city came a crow,
With my travels vying,
Round my head as on I go,
To this day he's flying.

Crow, oh, crow—thou capricious beast!
Wilt thou leave me never?
Swooping on me, as thy feast,
Would'st my flesh dissever?

Far upon my walking stave
I shall not be wending;
Faithful, then, until the grave,
Let that be my ending.

Der Tod und das Mädchen

Das Mädchen:

Vorüber, ach, vorüber!
Geh', wilder Knochenmann!
Ich bin noch jung, geh' lieber!
Und rühre mich nicht an.

Der Tod:

Gib deine Hand, du schön und zart Gebild!
Bin Freund und komme nicht zu strafen.
Sei gutes Muts! Ich bin nicht wild,
Sollst sanft in meinen Armen schlafen!

Matthias Claudius
(Franz Schubert)

Death and the Maiden

Maiden:

Begone now, oh, begone now—
Old specter, fierce to see;
I am still young, move on now,
Withhold your touch from me.

Death:

Give me thy hand, thou lovely shape and mild!
Thy friend, I chastise not nor cumber.
Be not afraid, I am not wild,
In my arms softly shalt thou slumber!

Die Männer sind méchant

Du sagtest mir es, Mutter:
Er ist ein Springinsfeld!
Ich würd' es dir nicht glauben,
Bis ich mich krank gequält!
Ja, ja, nun ist er's wirklich;
Ich hatt' ihn nur verkannt!
Du sagtest mir's, o Mutter,
Du sagtest mir's, o Mutter:
Die Männer sind méchant!

Vor'm Dorf, im Busch, als gestern
Die stille Dämm'rung sank,
Da rauscht' es: „Guten Abend!"
Da rauscht' es: „Schönen Dank!"—
Ich schlich hinzu, ich horchte,
Ich stand wie fest gebannt,
Er war's, mit einer Andern,
Er war's, mit einer Andern:
Die Männer sind méchant!

O Mutter, welche Qualen!
Es muß heraus, es muß!
Es blieb nicht bloß beim Rauschen,
Es blieb nicht bloß beim Gruß!
Vom Gruße kam's zum Kusse;
Vom Kuße zum Druck der Hand;
Vom Druck, ach liebe Mutter!
Vom Druck, ach liebe Mutter . . . !
Die Männer sind méchant!

Johann Seidl
(Franz Schubert)

The Men Are a Bad Lot

Oh, Mother, yes, you said to me,
"He is a good-for-naught."
I scarcely could believe it
Till in his torments caught.
Alas, he is that surely,
It seems I knew him not;
You told me, dearest Mother,
You told me, dearest Mother—
The men are a bad lot!

Within the town copse, yesterday
Just as the twilight came,
I heard a soft "Good evening!"
Then, "Thanks—to you the same."
In silence I stole nearer
And stared, glued to the spot—
It was he with another,
It was he with another—
The men are a bad lot!

Oh, Mother, guess my torment—
It must come out, come out!
It did not stop at greetings,
Or whispers round about;
From there it went to kissing,
To hand-clasps quick and hot,
From clasp of hands, oh, Mother,
From clasp of hands, oh, Mother—
The men are a bad lot!

Kommen und Scheiden

So oft sie kam, erschien mir die Gestalt
So lieblich wie das erste Grün im Wald.

Und was sie sprach, drang mir zum Herzen ein
Süß wie des Frühlings erstes Lied (im Hain).

Und als Lebwohl sie winkte mit der Hand,
War's, ob der letzte Jugendtraum mir schwand.

Nikolaus Lenau
(Robert Schumann)

Approaching and Departing

Whene'er she came, her form appeared to me
Enchanting, as when woodland buds burst free.

And what she said, heart-piercing every word
Sweet as when spring's first song is heard.

And as farewell, with flutt'ring hand she said,
Oh, then, methought that youth's last dream had fled.

Zueignung

Ja, du weißt es, teu're Seele
Daß ich fern von dir mich quäle,
Liebe macht die Herzen krank,
Habe Dank!

Einst hielt' ich des Freiheit Zecher
Hoch den amethysten Becher,
Und du segnetest den Trank,
Habe Dank!

Und beschwörst darin die Bösen
Bis ich—was ich nie gewesen—
Heilig, heilig ans Herz dir sank—
Habe Dank!

Hermann von Gilm
(Richard Strauss)

Dedication

Yes, dear soul, you know it surely,
Far from you I suffer sorely,
Love-sick hearts require love's cures,
Thanks be yours!

Once I raised the purpling beaker,
Freedom's most inebriate seeker.
And you blest the drink that lures—
Thanks be yours!

Banned therein all harms forever,
Till I—consecrated as never—
Heart to heart pledged what love ensures—
Thanks be yours!

Bois épais, redouble ton ombre,
Tu ne saurais être assez sombre;
Tu ne peux trop cacher mon malheureux amour.

Je sens un désespoir, dont l'horreur est extrême!
Je ne dois plus voir ce que j'aime,
Je ne veux plus souffrir le jour.

Philippe Quinault
(Jean-Baptiste Lully)

Dusky Woods

Dusky woods, thy shadows redouble,
Though dark, thou cans't not hide the trouble,
I hide not nor remove,
Of my unhappy love.

Despair and horror say
That my fear is to lose her,
'Twere so, mine eye that pursues her
Could no more bear the light of day.

Grace Notes after Translating Poetry

Traditore—Traduttore! This Italian antithesis, as curt and explosive as a curse, has too long cast a lean, bilious shadow over one branch of the writer's activity: translation. Before I proceed to set down some convictions that have sprung up after an over-long, exhausting, yet exhilarating task of translation, I want to question myself and my readers as to the truth of this dictum. If the original piece of writing that needs to be translated is a dull but perhaps useful bit of information; if it be a factual account, let us say, of scientific experimentation; or pedestrian passages of journalism, does a translator knowing both languages need do more than make a literal transcript of one language into the other? Himself not inspired, but having to earn his living, has he injured or demoted the first writer? I think not. No more than if he has moved some furniture from one room into another.

The question arises: How did men begin to translate at all? Must not this faculty given by the grace of the Logos— secularly described as the logical principle in the universe— occur in this wise, whether to a savage or a savant?

The creature, Man, begins to look about his world. However, after he looks he will be able to see, and when he sees long enough he will perceive. Then if he has any vital curiosity, he begins to compare, to relate what he has seen and perceived. Naturally, it follows almost unconsciously that the reflection called meditation comes into being. With meditation comes the urge to communicate. Men need to know each other. When communication becomes urgent, the desire for a written language is felt.

Of course animals, and also men, have other means of communication, but language is the bond that is most capable of widespread communication and the *Word* has had enormous power, for good and for evil. Since the *Word* became recognizable in our universe, it has been one of the most powerful means of enlightening men, giving them a new instrument—an instrument that is an addition to thinking and doing. I knew the whispers of conscience at an early age. Beginning at eight years of age, I felt a compulsion to perform any and all tasks with excellence. By this self-imposed discipline, I built up my self-respect. After the age of fifty, the completion of a long, heartbreakingly difficult but absorbing assignment of translation implanted in me the conviction that what is mandatory for translating a writing, which one could call a work of art, is the following state of mind.

For the last fifty years at least, nearly everyone has realized that in each human being there are both the female and the male components, whether this individual be a man or a woman. It seems to me more advantageous for the translator if he has a larger feminine component than a masculine one. That does not mean that the translator must be either man or woman but that the female characteristics should be uppermost and strongest. For the essence of the feminine nature is to be submissive; the greatest task of the female, at least so nature has arranged it, is for her to promote the race. Therefore, when she knows that she will become a mother she should submit every other impulse of her being to the great task she has in view: everything must be subservient to the bearing of the child. However, in substituting (for the sake of this argument) translator for mother—the builder, the bearer, and the nourisher of the new being—the translator of a work of art must feel the same subservience. The translator subjugates the ego in order to master the poem.

As I have said in another context: The first axiom of translation is for the translator to be translated. He becomes *it*. A translator makes himself identical or is made identical with the work of art. For the time being there is no other identity. This is a very absorbing experience. It is the same kind of total submission that a mother has to her task and there is no other: the great work is simply to perfect the task. This is the attitude of prayer. We pray with faith but we are never sure of the outcome. Only time will tell. And how much time will we be granted?

There are a few practical hints. One takes for granted that the translator knows both languages. Of greater importance is that he knows all the resources of his mother-tongue and exercises it as a natural and joyous gift. Its beauty nourishes him. In using it well, he becomes exhilarated and often exalted. But when it comes to a foreign language, he must also strive to use it as a native. That is, he must be on the lookout for idioms. I know of several amusing incidents when the ignorance of the idiom betrayed the translator to ludicrousness.

One woman who admitted that her German was *"fließend aber schlecht"* (fluent but faulty) in translating a novel dealing with an orthodox Jewish family, translated the word *Schmalz* as "bacon." She could have learned from one of her several husbands that her translation of *Schmalz* as "bacon" had more than one offensive connotation.

Another instance: a man of letters, novelist, translator, university professor, translated *Die Dame* as "Our Lady," thereby giving a sacerdotal meaning to what in the story was an innocent little girl's vision of a lovely woman. In this instance, readers with a pious or poetical inclination could argue that the novelist and his translator each did better than he knew. For, to the pure, unclouded feeling-nature of a child, the secular and the sacred may unite—intuition coupling the mind and heart.

A third example concerned a novel written of Napoleon's time in which a private or political betrayal was passed over without reproval or punishment. The German phrase was: *"Und kein Hahn krähte danach,"* and was literally translated "and no cock crowed." The translator was pardoned his ignorance because, being a Bible-reader, the betrayal here narrated was in his mind like Peter's betrayal of his Master, Jesus of Nazareth. But, idiomatically, the phrase is interpreted, "Nobody gave a hoot." Oh, yes, *traditore* may even innocently become *tradutore*.

But how lucky is the translator whose mother-tongue is our beautiful English language! It is so hospitable an ocean that it accepts the rivers of speech from nearly every land on earth—not only the European languages, but traces from the ancient Sanskrit and even Chinese and Japanese expressions as well. Once, for one of my classes, I contrived a little etymological exercise. Some linguists have agreed that my intuition was correct. Others argued that my knowledge was too limited. *Der Dichter* may have been derived from the Latin *dicere* (to speak out). Here it is:

In that classroom the study was poetry and how it is made. I always insisted that neither I nor anyone could *teach* a person to write poetry. *Poeta nascitur, non fit.* All I could do was to analyze all the forms in English poetry I knew, including the so-called French forms. Then, having explained the structure and read enough examples for the form to become familiar, I asked each student to write some verses in that form. It amazed me how often some pupil, not obviously a poet, became quickly proficient in mastering a form that took his fancy. At least, my students learned their craft.

Let us think about the word *poetry* and what takes place in a poet's mind.

In German the word for poet is *der Dichter*.

A poem is *das Gedicht*.

Poetry as a generic term is *die Dichtung*.

The adjectival root of these nouns is *dicht* (meaning dense), so a poet feeling the stirrings of inspiration knows it as a very insubstantial idea hovering in the empyrean and it "teases him into thought."

Poetry at its best is concrete. The abstract is a better playground for philosophers: their formulations are *their* kind of poetry. Blake said, "Poetry should consist of 'minute particulars.'" Poetry before it takes shape is as featureless as a tiny blob of protoplasm in embryo. It is a floating idea, a kind of colored music not yet a melody, a rainbow speck in the air that often floats beyond the grasp of mind. An "airy nothing" needing a "habitation and a name." So the poet as a *Dichter* makes his bubble *dicht* (dense) enough to be seized as matter—something concrete. As matter, the material brain then transmutes it again so that it can be received into the mind and heart. This is *transubstantiation*—"the Word made flesh"—and the spirit receives it back into its immaterial but immortal form.

As a parting gift, I ventured to define what Edwin Arlington Robinson said of poetry: that it is "indefinable but unmistakable."

Poetry is the testament of imaginative living.

Testament is a writing that may mean either a witness or a legacy.

Imagination is the movement of the mind toward reality (whether visible or invisible).

Fantasy is the movement of the mind toward unreality.

Therefore, one might say that Imagination is structural and Fantasy is decorative. But as a maker (for the poet was originally known as The Maker), a producer rather than a creator—there is only one Creator—he must be careful not to use too much decoration until he is sure that the structure is strongly built on a firm foundation.

Lastly, a man is often characterized by his walk and gestures, his rhythm. In translating a poem try to catch the rhythm—the inner movement—even if you cannot duplicate the rhymes. All poetry is not rhymed but verse without rhythm is not poetry. This is the fuel that feeds my fire. May a flying spark ignite another's blaze.

Envoi

In calling this varied and disparate collection of translations, *Re-Creations,* I do not imply that they often depart from the original texts. This happens rarely and only when in the song, in the mating of words and music, the latter dominated and demanded a slight preference. Not infrequently, great composers have lent their genius to a text on a level lower than their music—yet, in many, many instances, this marriage turned into a couple of rare charm.

These poems came to my notice more by chance than design. That they came to be a book was a matter also of happenstance. Impelled by caprice, I translated them at odd times over a number of years. They were slipped into a file and more or less forgotten. In short, they were recreations. At times, I would remember a verse learned, perhaps, in adolescence. Sometimes, a friend would copy out a favorite bit of verse and ask me to translate it. After I had passed the test of trying to bring the intricate thought and serpentine sentences of Hermann Broch's *The Death of Virgil* into the English language (and, by a miracle, succeeding), some of my friends thought I could translate anything. I never made a secret of the fact that I had begun that major task as a neophyte, but the result has often been called "masterly." However, I did discover in myself the infinite capacity for taking pains. The reward has been wholly subjective: I myself find deep pleasure in any enterprise that seems to be well done and worth the doing.

A great many of the poems found here, I learned through the study of music and the short professional career as a lieder-singer that followed after fifteen arduous years of preparation. The songs I sang in concert and in private have never left me. I still remember a vast number in German, old Italian, early French and English—as well as many Negro spirituals. Over a span of years, I translated a few of these songs, again selected by chance . . . songs that can be sung as easily in English as in their original languages.

List of Authors Translated

Günther Anders	1907–
Charles Baudelaire	1821–1867
Richard Beer-Hofmann	1866–1945
Uriel Birnbaum	1894–1956
Bertolt Brecht	1898–1956
Hermann Broch	1886–1951
Matthias Claudius	1740–1815
Hermann von Gilm	1812–1864
Johann Wolfgang von Goethe	1749–1832
Heinrich Heine	1797–1856
Paul Heyse	1830–1914
Friedrich Hölderlin	1770–1843
Judah Karni	1884–1949
Jean de La Fontaine	1621–1695
Karl von Lemcke	1831–1913
Nikolaus Lenau	1802–1850
Rudolf Leonhard	1889–1953
Eduard Mörike	1804–1875
Christian Morgenstern	1871–1914
Wilhelm Müller	1794–1827
Friedrich Wilhelm Nietzsche	1844–1900
Philippe Quinault	1635–1688
Hans Sahl	1902–
Johann Seidl	1804–1875
Ludwig Uhland	1787–1862
Johannes Urzidil	1896–

List of Composers

Johannes Brahms	1833–1897
Jean-Baptiste Lully	1632–1687
Anton Rubinstein	1829–1894
Franz Schubert	1797–1828
Robert Schumann	1810–1856
Richard Strauss	1864–1949
Hugo Wolf	1860–1903